I0004926

blurb

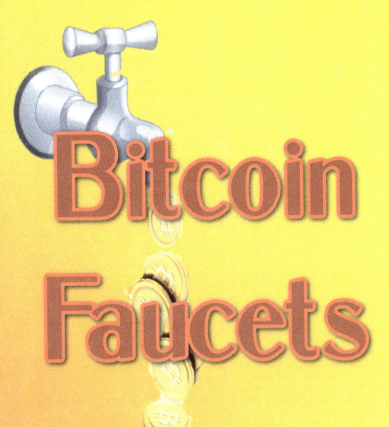

Bitcoin Faucets

Quick Introduction

If you are new to collecting Bitcoin or you are well on your way...

Bitcoin is a digital currency which operates free of any central control.

There is 100 million satoshis to one bitcoin.

It is named after Satoshi Nakamoto, the creator/s of the protocol used in blockchains and the bitcoin cryptocurrency.

Blockchains move the currency around safely.

Many people can buy bitcoin or they can play games, PTC (Paid to click) view ads to earn Satoshis and more. Earn free satoshi from faucets.

People bank their satoshi's into mini wallets and wallets.

Bitcoin can be used to buy things online or exchange many things and even normal cash.

Always be careful and checkout sites before handing any money over.

The best advice is Don't invest in any website which promises to multiply your money or give you a certain percentage of profit daily.

Be careful not to invest in any ponzi schemes. Be careful when sending money to someone else.
Basically there are plenty of sites where you can collect free Satoshis without risking your own money.

Bitcoin is not a quick money scheme.

** read plenty of sites and learn lots.

In this booklet we have listed some sites to get you earning free Satoshis to start you off.

Once you have set yourself up with some faucets, then start looking for a wallet to put your cryptocurrency into. One with extra security would be best. - CoinJar is good or Bitcoin Wallets can help you to find the right one for you...

CoinJar
https://cjr.io/heGK

Earns 500 CoinJar Points when you join.

There is also this site to check out

Bitcoin Wallets
https://bitcoin.com.au

Coin Types

Coin Types

Bitcoin

Ethereum

Dogecoin

Litecoin

Bitcoin Cash

Dash

DigiByte

Tron

Tether TRC20

Feyorra

Zcash

Binance BEP20

Solana

plus many others

Contents

Crypto-Tab-Browser

Crypto-Tab-Browser

Referral Link
https://cryptotabbrowser.com/5800392

Free to join with options to upgrade

Mines Bitcoin automatically and in the
background.

Withdrawal minimum is 0.00001
to your crypto-wallet

Earn more with mining networks and
Cloud Boost Mining

Info includes
Your Balance
Mined by you
Mining by your network
Total Earnings

CryptoTab is the youngest browser among all the major browsers in the world, and already more than 25 million users. CryptoTab is the first and only browser in the world with built-in mining. No investments needed! Try it right now and earn your first BTC with CryptoTab Browser!

I normally run my CryptoTab on a separated computer and then that way I can still use google to search other things.

The CryptoTab Browser is basic format.

With CryptoTab, it also mines even when the computer is off - (not as much as when it is on, but it still mines for you)

Faucets

Faucet Pay

Referral Link
https://faucetpay.io/?r=1794749

Earn, receive, send, play, and exchange cryptocurrencies like Bitcoin, Doge, Litecoin, Ethereum and much more for free, directly from your FaucetPay wallet.

Faucet pay has many options for earning Satoshi

Earn from...
Faucet List

Offer-wall

Surveys

Paid to click

FEY Staking

Plus Affiliate Programme

Collectible Coins

Bitcoin

Ethereum

Dash

Dogecoin

Tron

Litecoin

Tether

Bitcoin Cash

Fcyorra

Digibyte

All coins can be converted to other coins once reached minimums.

EarnBitMoon

Referral Link

https://earnbitmoon.club/?ref=119244

Earn every 5 minutes

You register with an email and password.

Check your emails to activate it.

It will take you to the page and then you can log in.

Once in...

On the left side will be your account details, what you have earn and the level you are at.

There is an option to either use the basic (free) one or pay for high chances.

In the middle will be where you earn coins.

(Claim Free coins every 5 minutes) Under this when ready it will say Roll Now - Grab Jackpot. Click on this link when it appears. and follow instructions. Cash-out is minimum $0.20

Paid to click

Ad views

Achievements & Stats

Levels 1 - 34, with a counter that counts down to get to the next level.

Satoshi Hero

Referral Link
https://satoshihero.com/en/register?r=5jeeb58j

Satoshi Hero is a funny character we've created for you to make the process of getting free money from us more fun.

Every half hour get option to spin the wheel of fortune for free to collect Satoshi's or pay for higher amounts.
To collect amount click on truck pictures etc.

Offer-wall and games plus quick surveys to collect Satoshi.
Cash out at 30,000 Satoshi.

Claim Free Coins

Referral Link

https://claimfreecoins.io/free-bitcoin/?
r=1QCeC6DvieM7JESCbQ7iJCn7kZksCRXXhs

Log in with your deposit link from Faucet Pay to claim free Bitcoin every 5 minutes.

Refresh to claim and Login then click continue.

A box will come up.

Tick I am not a robot and click the 4 links in the corners, in order from the top.

Then click Verify.

Your free Satoshi will be sent to your Faucet pay account.

Other features are available.

Bitcoin Faucets

Neobits

Referral Link
https://neobits.net/?r=27658

Manual faucet, every 5 minutes
follow instructions to claim

Auto-faucet
PTC (paid to click)
Short links
Claims per day
and more

Need 99 exp to level up
Minimum withdrawal is 50 tokens
to your Faucet Pay mini wallet

Has counter to count down to what you can
do in a 24 hour period.

To the moon Faucet

Manual faucet

Approx. 40 token every 5 minutes.

Auto-faucet

Mining

Short-links

PTC

Lottery

Tasks

Offerwall

Dice and more

Withdrawal

Minimum 100000 tokens

into Litecoin, Bitcoin and more

Multicoins

Referral Link
https://multicoins.net/?r=67263

Earn free coins every five minutes.
then solve the security link.

Manual faucet

Auto faucet

offer-wall

Dice

PTC

Lottery

Faucet-Pay withdrawal

and more

Withdrawing coin choice

Bitcoin Faucetpay
Bitcoin Expresscrypto
Monero Expresscrypto
Tether Faucetpay
Litecoin Expresscrypto
Litecoin Faucetpay
Reddcoin Expresscrypto
Payeer USD
Tron Faucetpay
Feyorra FaucetPay

Minimum withdrawal is 0.1 USD

Coin-Pot

Referral Link
https://coinpot.in/?r=83843

Daily Bonus
Offerwall
PTC
Shortlinks

Varying withdrawal limits per coinage.

SolPay

https://solpay.in/

Earn through Faucet
every five minutes
Games
Tasks
PTC
Shortlinks
Level Bonus
and more

Minimum payout 0.0001

Adsbitly

https://adsbitly.com/?r=1340

Manual Faucet every 5 minutes

Auto Faucet

Wheel of Fortune

Dice

Achievement

Shortlinks

PTC

plus more

Withdrawal min. 1000 tokens

FireFaucet

Varying minimums
Earn every 20 minutes

Shortlinks

Surveys

Faucet

Offerwall

Tasks

PTC

Bitcoin

Binance BEP20

Tether TRC20

Ethereum

Dogecoin

Litecoin

Dash

Tron

Nano

And more

Golden Clix

https://www.goldenclix.com/

Earn by

Watching Ads

Simple Tasks

Surveys

Minimum payout $0.15

Questionable

Questionable faucets, you just have to be careful with these one. Some will require you to do a lot of work for minimum to no return. The best thing to do is to check them out before getting to serous. I am not saying they are no good, just check out if they are going to be useful to you.

Crazy Faucet

https://crazyfaucet.xyz/

This one is a ad base faucet, you put your FaucetPay Address in and don't forget to click the "I'm Not a Robot. and then follow instructions.

But you have to go through hoops to collect any, so just be careful with this one.

Crazy Faucet if for Litecoin.

you can earn one or two satoshi's at a time.

Dogecoin Faucet

Referral Link

https://doge-faucet.com/?
r=DKtD7uFw1Bed3WFr29zCEiVyQMuw4neSPF

I found this one gave decent Dogecoin, once I had worked through all the links

The best thing is before getting to involved with some, check them out.

You can still earn coins/tokens with these.

you have to put your FaucetPay address in to get you started and then work through advertisement pages for insurances.

Other Links

Other Links

Pasino
https://pasino.com

My Crypto Faucet
https://mycryptofaucet.eu/

Coinadster
https://coinadster.com/

5min-btc
https://5min-btc.ru/

Bybit
https://www.bybit.com/

Claimtrx
https://claimtrx.com/

Xfaucet
https://xfaucet.net/

Bigashbonus
https://bigdashbonus.ga/

Bitzcoin
https://bitzcoin.org/

Bitcoin Faucets

Ethiomi
https://ethiomi.com/

Ltcclick
https://www.ltcclick.com/

Faucetzoid
https://faucetzoid.online/

888satoshi
https://888satoshis.com/

Xfaucet
https://xfaucet.net/

Mixbits
https://mixbits.io/

Author's Other Books

Author's Other Books

Genealogy Made Easy
https://au.blurb.com/ebooks/605105-genealogy-made-easy
Softcover: *ISBN: 9781366710710*
Hardcover, Dust Jacket: *ISBN: 9781366710703*
Hardcover, ImageWrap: *ISBN: 9781366710727*
PDF: *https://au.blurb.com/b/7566791-genealogy-made-easy*

Knock, Knock
https://au.blurb.com/b/10262181-knock-knock
Softcover: ISBN: 9781715371364
Hardcover, Dust Jacket: ISBN: 9781715371371
Hardcover, ImageWrap: ISBN: 9781715371357

Essence

ebook : https://www.blurb.com/ebooks/763907-essence

Softcover ISBN: 9781006420085

Hardcover, Dust Jacket ISBN: 9781006420092

Hardcover, ImageWrap ISBN: 9781006419942

PDF : https://www.blurb.com/b/10877372-essence

The Genealogist Devotional

ebok: https://www.blurb.com/ebooks/766241-the-genealogist-devotional

Softcover ISBN: 9781006270574

Hardcover, Dust Jacket ISBN: 9781006270598

Hardcover, ImageWrap ISBN: 9781006270581

PDF: https://www.blurb.com/b/10926441-the-genealogist-devotional

Index

Links work at time of printing.

www.ingramcontent.com/pod-product-compliance
Lightning Source LLC
Chambersburg PA
CBHW041635050326
40689CB00024B/4967